Look on the Bright Side

A 31-DAY DEVOTIONAL TO FINDING JOY ON YOUR JOURNEY

Heather Bourne & Barbara Westmaas

Bourne Blessed Book
Group

Bourne Blessed Book
G r o u p

Heather Bourne
Bourne Blessed Books
Printed in the United States of America
First Printing 2020
First Edition 2020

Editor Ta-ning Conner

Dedication

I thank God for His goodness and mercy and for blessing me with this wonderful life. This book is dedicated to my children, (Nicole, Mack, & Heather), my son "in loves" (Jay & Christopher) and grandchildren, (Heaven, Ellington, Savannah & Christopher, Jr.). You all have been the fan club cheering me on and are such a great inspiration to me. I love you all!

I want to thank my husband, Mark, for his patience as I spent many hours working with Heather to bring this vision to light. I have enjoyed every minute of this journey co-writing this book with Heather, who brings out the Bright Side in me.

Love, Babs

Dedication

I dedicate this book to my Lord and Savior, Jesus Christ, who has been so faithful in my life. I commit to let my light shine so that He may be glorified!

To Momma Babs, my cheerleader of life long dreams! Your humility, strength, love, faith, beauty, humor, and compassion for all people has made me who I am today. I am grateful for the example. I love you, Momma Babs.

To my Husband, Chris, the man of my dreams and my best friend, you amaze me more everyday. When God blessed me to be your wife, He gave me the very best. Your love and support have made me confident to pursue my purpose. I love you...forever your rib.

To Savannah and Chris Jr., my two precious treasures. You bring me more joy and laughter than I could have ever hoped for! Being your Mommy is the greatest reward. I love you both.

To my siblings Nicole and Mack, the "Hodges Hustlers." We started at the bottom & now we're here. I am inspired daily by your greatness. You set the bar high for your little sister so that I would never settle on running the family toy store. I love you both.

And to my amazing SBC family, your love, loyalty, support and faith in your First family is second to none. We Love you. Our greatest days are ahead!

Love, Heather

Table of Contents

Intro

Be The Light

Matthew 5:16
Let your light so shine before men, that they may see your good works and glorify your Father in heaven.

During our world's darkest hour, The COVID-19 crisis, Mom and I were keeping the faith… but from a distance! Like many of you, we were separated from our loved ones while on quarantine lockdown, but we stayed connected to **The** one who has the master key. Through phone calls, email correspondence and zoom chats, our mother-daughter bond deepened as we partnered to write this book, in hopes of encouraging the world with hope, and humor during one of our darkest hours!

Sometimes when we are in a difficult season of life, we feel like we've been buried…but you have not been buried; you have actually just been planted. Great promises are about to sprout up and bloom in your life if you will simply believe it and receive it. Jesus is the light of the world, and since we have His light shining bright within us, we have the power to change the atmosphere and brighten things up a bit, by using our gifts to illuminate the darkness in the world. Just turn on the news for a few minutes, and you will be reminded of all the things that we could easily be discouraged about: The overall devastation of the Coronavirus pandemic, surviving quarantine, nations divided by politics, unemployment at an all-time high, struggling businesses, financial hardship, police brutality, racism, the homeless epidemic, poverty, hunger, mental health challenges and all sorts of issues. Seriously, what planet are we on?!

Things may appear to be dark and grim even for those who believe in God and walk by faith. It makes it difficult to navigate around all this negative stuff and simply live our best life. Even so, the scripture reminds us in **Matthew 5:16,** *Let your light so shine before men, that they may see your good works and glorify your Father in heaven.* Our light doesn't make bad things in the world stop happening, and it won't make our difficulties go away; BUT if we shine our bright light on them, Jesus can give us a different perspective and cause us to view things from where He's sitting. He's got the best seat in the house! He's seated at the right hand of God with ALL power in His hands, and He can make all things new.

"Like what?" you ask. A new perspective, new outlook, new peace of mind, newfound joy, new opportunities, a new car! (Wayment, this is not a name it & claim it book, lol!) But we do have that crazy faith to believe that the glass is never half empty, but always half full. All we must do is just turn on those lights… Click!

Now that you have your lights shining and your glass is raised half-full and ready to toast to the bright life, this is where this handy little book comes in. Each and every day, we encourage you to find joy on your journey through memory scriptures, real-life inspirational stories, gratitude journal pages and even a few cool song lyrics to brighten your day! We are here to cheer you on every day and remind you how amazing you are. Just like the lyrics tell us in Rihanna's song, "Diamonds", we gotta remember to, "Shine bright like a diamond…we're the beautiful ones in the sky." (Thanks, RiRi!)

Babs & Heather

Prayer: Dear Lord, let me never forget that I am the light of the world. It is my desire to shine brightly before others, allowing my attitude, words, and actions to reflect the values of Jesus. I want my life to be a testimony to Your goodness. In Jesus name, Amen.

Day 1

Cheer Up

Proverbs 17:22
A merry heart does good, like medicine, but a broken spirit dries the bones.

Fun Fact: The original title of this book was going to be, "Cheer Up!" but like any smart boss lady, I decided to run this title idea by a few trusted friends so that I could decide if the title was a good fit. One friend said, "When people tell me to 'Cheer Up,' it makes me feel similar to when people tell me to 'Calm down' or 'Relax.' It gets me so agitated that I want to start turning over tables as Jesus did in the temple!" Well, this response sealed the deal that "Cheer Up" was not my winning title. Her honest response made me laugh out loud. A good friend will tell you the truth and make you crack up laughin' in the same breath.

The Bible tells us in **Proverbs 17:22** , *A merry heart does good, like medicine, but a broken spirit dries the bones.* Not only does laughter reduce stress, but it also lowers your blood pressure, gives you an excellent ab workout, and releases endorphins. God wants us to laugh more, and He also desires for us to have joy. The word JOY is mentioned in the scriptures over 200 times. A little word, but of great significance. God wants us to discover how to have authentic joy in every season, even when we're going through difficult times.

Can you remember the last time you had a really good laugh? I admire my husband's ability to have a huge belly laugh almost every single day; whether he's watching tv or receiving a funny text from a friend, he really enjoys belting out a huge chuckle and, cheering himself up without the assistance of anyone else. Trust me though, those daily, super loud outbursts of joy can easily teeter toward being both annoying and inspiring all at the same time! But deep down inside, ya' gotta love it!

I always know when my husband is on the phone with one particular cousin. Once they start clowning and laughing and telling loud stories, I know immediately who he is in cahoots with. He gets off the phone, and I say, "How's Kenny?" And my husband is always tickled that I never get it wrong! God loves you, and He wants you to laugh loud and live long, so intentionally surround yourself with people who will cheer you up and cheer you on! We all need a Cousin Kenny in our lives.

Heather

Prayer: Dear Lord, I pray that Your joy would fill my heart and strengthen my soul. I pray that times of joyful laughter would replace those seasons of weeping and hardship. In Jesus name, Amen.

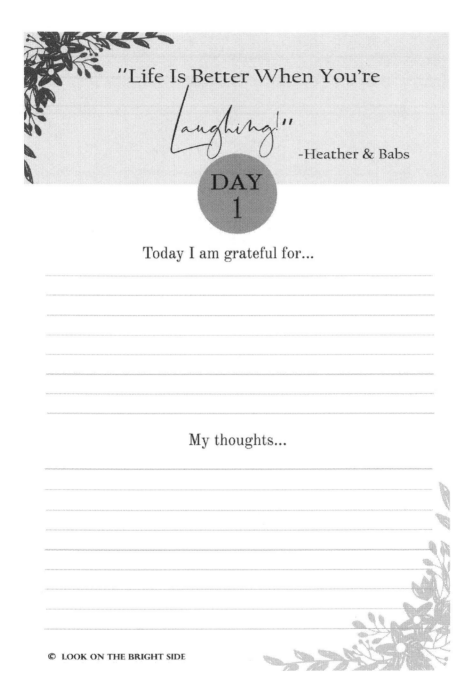

"Life Is Better When You're

Laughing!"

-Heather & Babs

**DAY
1**

Today I am grateful for...

My thoughts...

Day 2

Switchin' Channels

Matthew 6:34
Therefore do not worry about tomorrow, for tomorrow will worry about its own things. Sufficient for the day is its own trouble.

Bob Marley had many classic songs during his career, yet there's one hit that makes us feel more relaxed than the rest. The lyrics in "Three Little Birds" say, "Don't worry about a thing, because every little thing is gonna be all right...." The musical genius once revealed during a magazine interview that what became one of his most notable lyrics started off as a message he received from three little birds that frequently landed on his porch in Kingston, Jamaica. Who would have thought that those sweet little birds would inspire Marley to write such a classic song known all over the world!

Did you ever stop to think about what a waste of time it is to worry? Well, it is! When we worry, we are essentially telling God that our focus is on our fears instead of Him. He wants to turn your valley of battles into a valley of blessings, this requires us to have faith over our fears. If we prayed about our problems as much as we worried about them, we would have much less to worry about! (say that to yourself three times until it really sinks in!)

Prayer changes things, but worrying is worthless! **Matthew 6:34** reads, ***Therefore, do not worry about tomorrow, for tomorrow will worry about its own things. Sufficient for the day is its own trouble.*** Every time I am tempted to worry, I train my brain to switch from fear to faith and from worry to worship. It's like switching channels on your television from one network to another.

When I was a little girl growing up in Detroit in the 70s, I would visit my Grandma Alma's house almost every weekend. Back then, there was no such thing as a wireless tv remote control like we have today. Grandma would tell me to get up, take a long walk over to the television and change the channel by hand. I was her human remote! I remember falling asleep on the couch often, but when Saturday Night Live was about to come on, Grandma would say, "Get up and switch the channel." I didn't feel like it, but I got up and turned that knob with a quickness. Every time you feel worry creeping into your thoughts, you gotta get up (mentally) and change the channel… switch from fear to faith! I've learned that worrying does not take away tomorrow's troubles, it takes away today's peace.

Heather

> **Prayer: Dear Lord, allow my faith to outweigh my fears, reminding me that worry adds nothing to my life. Thank You for being a very present help to me today. In Jesus name, Amen.**

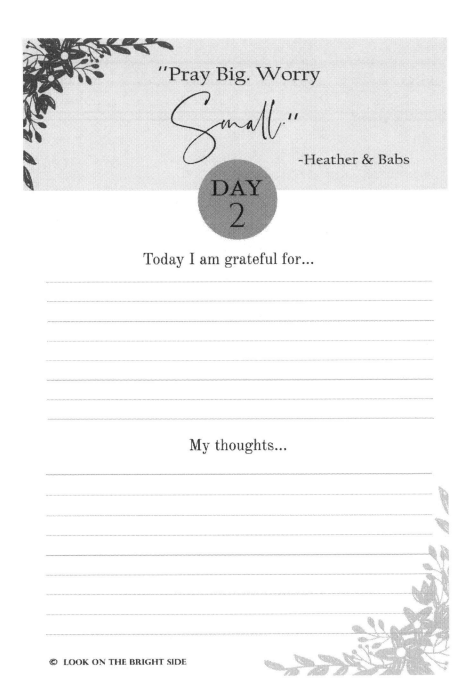

"Pray Big. Worry *Small.*"

-Heather & Babs

DAY 2

Today I am grateful for...

My thoughts...

© LOOK ON THE BRIGHT SIDE

Day 3
An Ought Against Oprah

Mark 11:25
And whenever you stand praying, if you have anything
against anyone, forgive him, that your Father in heaven
may also forgive you your trespasses.

On my 70th birthday, I decided to treat myself to the ultimate gift…FORGIVENESS!   I will never forget how the Lord revealed to me that I had been holding a long-term grudge against Oprah, one that lasted for over 20 years! My daughter, Nicole, was graduating from Spelman College, and I could hardly wait to proudly watch my first-born walk across that stage and receive her degree. I got to campus very early because, with the one and only Oprah Winfrey as the keynote speaker, you could certainly expect there to be a jammed pack crowd! Hearing Oprah speak live was also a dream come true, and the idea that two incredible moments would be happening at once was just too much to even comprehend!

This was actually happening, and now when I look back on that time I can imagine Oprah on stage, yelling out to all the deserving graduates, "You get a degree! You get a degree! And You get a degree!" Well, I would never get to hear Oprah's inspirational words up close and personal, nor would I get to see my daughter walk across that stage to receive the degree she so deserved.

It turned out that the local news stations leaked Oprah's live appearance, and HUNDREDS of people crashed the ceremony uninvited, leaving no seats for most of us proud parents and other officially invited guests. I was so disappointed! And that's when I vowed never to watch the Oprah Winfrey Show ever again. Now, you may be thinking, "How petty to hold a grudge over that. How was that Oprah's fault?" Well, in my mind, all I knew was that I would have been able to see my baby grace the stage in her cap and, gown had it not been for Ms. O drawing such a tremendous crowd.

So yes, as ridiculous as it seemed, I blamed Oprah for missing one of the most monumental moments of my child's life. I thank God for both wisdom and 20/20 hindsight because I can see now just how silly that was. So, ok Oprah, all is forgiven!

The scripture reads in **Mark 11:25**, *And whenever you stand praying, if you have anything against anyone, forgive*

him, that your Father in heaven may also forgive you your trespasses.

Holding a grudge doesn't make us better, it makes us bitter, and forgiving doesn't make us weak, it sets us free! Forgiveness is one of the greatest gifts we can give to ourselves, and doing so gives us the opportunity to unwrap true freedom.

Babs

Prayer: Dear Lord, help me to let go of any grudges I have harbored against anyone. Allow me to show them Your love and allow me to move on to the great things You have in store for me today. In Jesus name, Amen.

"Forgiveness Doesn't Change The Past...It Changes The Future."

-Heather & Babs

DAY 3

Today I am grateful for...

_____
_____
_____
_____
_____
_____
_____

My thoughts...

_____
_____
_____
_____
_____
_____
_____

© LOOK ON THE BRIGHT SIDE

Day 4

Just Dance

Psalms 149:3
Let them praise His name with the dance; Let them sing
praises to Him with timbrel and harp.

I'm sure you've heard the phrase, "Dance like nobody's watching!" I just love the sentiment behind that idea, and I truly believe that if we all would just abandon our concerns about other people's opinions of us, we would totally free ourselves to really enjoy life, be more daring, and find out who we really are along the way. If we felt the urge to break out and dance in the streets like we were a part of a flash mob, or move and groove amongst the pews at church, it would be a very normal thing to do, and we wouldn't have to be the only one.

I remember when I surprised my mom and took her to the taping of the Ellen Show for her birthday. Before the show started, the stand-up comedian was having fun warming up the crowd and asked if anyone wanted to come down and dance. Before I knew it, Momma Babs had sprinted down to the main stage and was dancing to Pharrell's song,

"Happy!" Watching her experience so much joy put a big smile on my face. The audience started cheering her on. This made me giggle because my mother may be in her mid-70s, but she still keeps up with the latest dance trends. Just ask her about the Renegade dance…she's up for the challenge.

Not only should we incorporate more dance into our everyday lives, but it should also be a part of our expressions of appreciation to God during church services. I love to lift my hands and dance before the Lord during Sunday worship. There are times when I look around and see many people sitting down during praise and worship. I was taught that we stand to praise God, we sit to learn, and we kneel to pray!

Psalms 149:3, reads, *Let them praise His name with the dance; Let them sing praises to Him with timbrel and harp.* Now you can see from the scripture that it's God's idea and not mine. We all know His ideas work every time! So, when it comes to praising God, even when we don't feel like it, we need to press our way through and do it anyway. Our deliverance is in our praise. Our healing is in our praise. Our breakthroughs are in our praise. Remember, there are two times to praise God…When you feel like it…AND when you don't!

Heather

> *Prayer: Dear Lord, please give me the boldness to dance, the boldness to praise, and the boldness to express my heart toward You, whether it's in private or in front of people. Thank You for Your Holy Spirit, which gives me boldness when I worship. In Jesus name, Amen.*

"Dance And Be

Free."

-Heather & Babs

DAY
4

Today I am grateful for...

_____
_____
_____
_____
_____
_____
_____

My thoughts...

_____
_____
_____
_____
_____
_____
_____

Day 5

Self-Care Isn't Selfish

Genesis 2:2
And on the seventh day God ended His work which He had done, and He rested on the seventh day from all His work which He had done.

I usually stay up too late every night only to realize it was a bad idea every morning. My son, Chris, likes to set his alarm for 6:15 am, and he is usually hovering over me, fully dressed by 6:30, requesting mini pancakes and to be dropped off to school as early as possible (like, as soon as they open the gates!) With the Monday thru Friday school routine and, early morning wakeups on Sundays for church service, I rarely get rest. There are many days when I say to myself, "Awake must be the new sleep!"

"Rest" is defined as "peace, ease or refreshment." "Relax" means "to become loose or less firm, to have a milder manner, to be less stiff." The Bible speaks quite highly of rest. It is a repeated theme throughout the scriptures, beginning with the creation week. **Genesis 2:2** reads, *And on the seventh day God ended His work which He had done,*

and He rested on the seventh day from all His work which He had done. God created for six days; then He rested, not because He was tired but to set the standard for us to follow.

As I get older, I realize that I am not invincible and just like babies get a lil' cranky when they skip nap time, I can see the importance of getting some good solid rest, so that I don't get burnt out and have a meltdown, or temper tantrum right when my family needs me the most! I remember flying out to Kansas for Thanksgiving holiday to visit my sister Nicole and family when I was struck by something the flight attendant instructed all passengers to do. She said, "In the event that there is a loss in cabin pressure, oxygen masks will drop from the compartment overhead. If you are traveling with a small child, please secure your own mask before helping those in need of extra assistance."

So, I'm thinking to myself, "should I call Child Protective Services on her? Is she saying to help *ourselves* before we help our children?" My first instinct would be to place the lifesaving oxygen mask onto my children before helping myself. But as I sit back and logically assess the instruction, I come to realize that there is a reason that we must place our own mask on first.

There is wisdom in having our own physical life secure before attempting to help others. It has taken me a while to get the revelation that taking care of ourselves is an important part of taking care of our loved ones. You are essential! After 12 years, I finally get it. So, what life lesson can we learn from the flight attendant's illustration? You can't pour from an empty cup. Be sure to take care of YOU first!

Heather

Prayer: Dear Lord, give me the wisdom to know when I need to rest. I pray that You will anoint me with strength and self-care today, tomorrow, and always. I pray that You will grace me with patience and wisdom. Help me, Father, to take care of myself so that I can take care of others. In Jesus name, Amen.

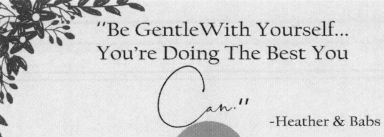

"Be Gentle With Yourself...
You're Doing The Best You

Can."

-Heather & Babs

DAY
5

Today I am grateful for...

My thoughts...

Day 6

The Three C's

Ecclesiastes 3:1
To everything there is a season, A time for every purpose under heaven.

Mama Said was the first book I wrote as a tribute to my mother, Alma Moore. In the book, I highlight many of the words of wisdom she taught me while growing up. Even into my later years, I always held on to the advice and wisdom I received from the woman who had plenty of it. I want to share with you the 3 C's of life that I learned from Mama, in hopes that they will help you as you leap out in faith and grab all of the wonderful opportunities that are headed your way.

#1. Choice... There is power in making a decision, and with guidance from the Lord, you can be sure to make the right one. But remember that even making no decision is actually a decision in and of itself, so it's better to just make up your mind and decide.

#2. Chance...You will only regret the chances you never take. Don't focus on the fear of the unknown, instead think about all the wonderful possibilities of what lies ahead. Make a choice today to take a chance and leap out in faith.

#3 Change...Change is good, but change certainly comes with many challenges! There are moments in life when a change will be overdue and quite necessary, and it will require you to come out of your comfort zone and do what you must do.

It's time to make a **Choice** to take a **Chance,** or your life will never **Change**!

Ecclesiastes 3:1 reads, *To everything there is a season, A time for every purpose under heaven.* I want to encourage you that a shift in God's favor is coming in this season. If you want something you never had, you must do something you've never done. Choice is about shifting your mindset. Chance is about challenging yourself to leave your comfort zone. Change is envisioning what is possible...not just what is. The greatest obstacle to your progress in life often comes from one single source...You! Step out in faith and do something great. Write that book, get your degree or start your business. You can do it. Strive for greatness, do something different and stand out. Get out of your own way!

Babs

> **Prayer: Dear Lord, You said that I would be transformed by the changing (or renewing) of my mind. Allow me to be open and willing to change that which no longer serves me. In Jesus name, Amen.**

"Step Out In

Faith."

-Heather & Babs

DAY
6

Today I am grateful for...

My thoughts...

Day 7

What's Joy Got to Do with It?

Psalms 28:7
The Lord is my strength and my shield; my heart trusted in Him, and I am helped; Therefore my heart greatly rejoices, And with my song I will praise Him.

My daughter's classmate, Skye, was 14 years old when she was diagnosed with a very rare form of cancer. When she received this devastating news, her faith kicked in immediately, and she just began to inspire us all with her smile, strength, and unspeakable joy in the midst of the battle. Skye underwent countless rounds of chemo, radiation, surgery, and biopsy procedures. When the doctors said there was nothing else they could do for her, an army of friends pitched in so that she and her family could take a private plane to a Boston hospital, to qualify for a medical trial treatment.

What a leap of faith! In the midst of the storm and even more reports from the doctors declaring that the medicine was not working against this aggressive cancer, the family kept their joy and continued to sing praises unto the Lord!

Although she was fighting for her life, God gave her strength and the faith to smile through the battle.

When we choose to give the fight over to the Lord, He rewards us with unlimited strength, faith, and a peace that surpasses all understanding. Joel Osteen once said, "Your attitude is going to determine your altitude. It will determine how high or how low you will go." Her smile and her joy inspired a #skyestrongtogether movement. She made a lasting impact on thousands of people by sharing her faith and unspeakable joy in the middle of this fight for her life. **Psalms 28:7** reads, *The Lord is my strength and my shield; my heart trusted in Him, and I am helped. Therefore my heart greatly rejoices, and with my song I praise Him.* When the Lord called Skye home, the lyrics to Kirk Franklin's gospel song entitled "Joy," took flight right there in the sanctuary where friends and family gathered to lay her to rest. The song says, "Joy…joy…God's great joy…joy…joy…down in my soul…Sweet, beautiful…soul saving joy…Ohhhhh joy joy…in my soul."

The pastor led hundreds of young friends, teachers and family to Christ that day by simply asking, "Do you want to experience the joy that Skye had, and see her again one day?" All those touched by Skye's spirit raised their hands and prayed the prayer of salvation that day. All glory to God for Skye's sweet, beautiful, soul-saving legacy of joy!

Heather

> **Prayer:** **Dear Lord, thank You for comforting me in seasons of sadness. You are near to the brokenhearted, and You save the crushed in spirit. You are my refuge and strength. In Jesus name, Amen.**

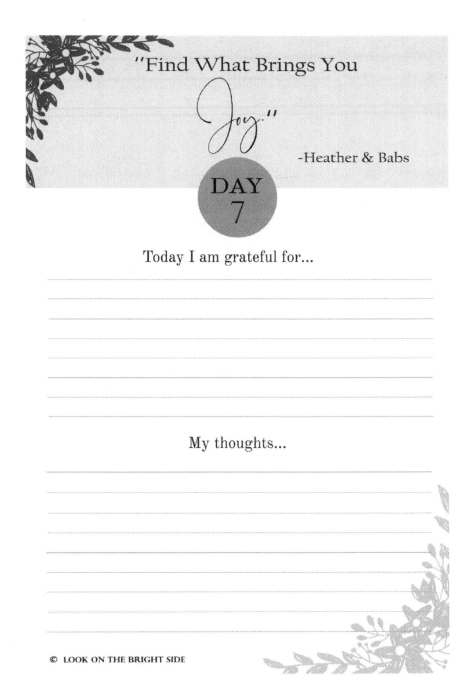

"Find What Brings You

Joy."

-Heather & Babs

DAY 7

Today I am grateful for...

My thoughts...

Day 8

Happily Ever After is a Choice

Psalms 118:8
It is better to trust in the Lord than to put confidence in man.

Cinderella met her prince at a ball, and when she ran home, he went searching for her with the glass slipper that fell off her foot. Then in 1988, another fairy tale themed movie, Coming to America (starring Eddie Murphy), hit the big screen. Prince Akeem, from the nation of Zamunda, came to America in hopes of finding his queen-to-be in Queens, NY. In both stories, they got married and they lived happily ever after.

I'm pretty sure I'm not the only one that grew up thinking that I would be swept up by the prince of my dreams, get married and live happily ever after. We all grow up and end up realizing that fairy tales give us an unrealistic picture of what being married will be like. A great marriage has many benefits, but it's not something that just happens; it requires some work. All couples go through some storms, our marriage is not exempt.

We tied the knot in November of 2004 in a fairy tale wedding (now that part really happened.) We were best friends and we got along extremely well. We waited almost three years before expanding our family, so we spent every day together taking walks, eating out, watching movies; we didn't have a care in the world!

After our daughter, Savannah, was born, it seemed like we started arguing about any and everything. We argued about finances. Chris is a saver, and I am a spender. I'm still working on that part. I was a new mom alone in the house for long hours with a newborn baby. I was overwhelmed with my new role as a mother and experiencing postpartum depression.

I practically lost all my friends because I just couldn't manage to keep up with them whenever they'd reach out. I was either too tired or too busy. That being the case, Chris and my mom were the only people I had to talk to or do anything with. I eventually learned that God is the only one who can supply all my needs. If I am unfulfilled, it is not because of my spouse, children, friends, or job. It's because I am not making God a priority and allowing Him to help me balance my life and emotions successfully. I was putting pressure on Chris to fill a space where only God belonged. **Psalms 118:8** reads, *It is better to trust in the Lord than to*

put confidence in man. That's exactly what I had to do in order to get the balance in my life that I so desperately needed. I thank the Lord that He gave Chris the grace and patience to ride these storms out by my side.

As I'm writing this book 15 years later, Chris is more than I asked for. Praise God for doing exceedingly and abundantly above all that I ask or think. We all want the fairy tale marriage, which is having a perfect mate without flaws and a perfect life without challenges. That is not reality. My husband is not perfect (many of you, including him, are shocked by reading this newsflash), but I can honestly say that he is the perfect person *for me.* I'd rather have him than any make believe prince from the fairytales.

Oh, and I am not perfect, either! I can be fussy when I'm hungry, bossy, messy *and* forgetful. Many people see me on Sunday mornings dressed up in my Sunday best, but catch me on an early Monday morning in the school carpool lane with wild hair- don't care, wearing Ugg boots and pajamas … It's not at all a fairytale. Here's the bottom line. Marriage takes prayer and work. It requires intentional effort. If you realize this at the beginning, you won't separate or divorce because of false expectations. Instead, when you go through trials and tribulations, believe that you are supposed to be with your mate, and be willing to do what it takes to make your marriage work. No relationship is all sunshine but two can share one umbrella and weather the storms together!

Heather

Prayer: Dear Lord, I pray over my marriage, asking that You infuse my husband and me with passion for life, passion for love, passion to grow in wisdom, and passion for serving You together in Jesus name, Amen.

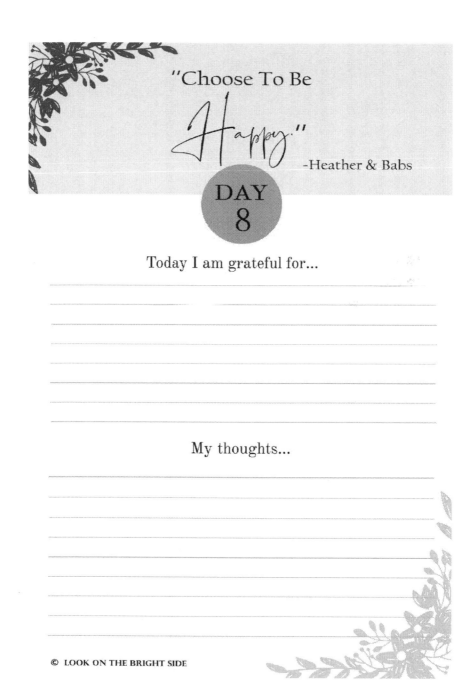

"Choose To Be

Happy."

-Heather & Babs

DAY
8

Today I am grateful for...

My thoughts...

Day 9

Faith Not Fear

2 Timothy 1:7
For God has not given us a spirit of fear, but of power and of love and of a sound mind.

In a Bible class, I was asked what was my earliest memory of having faith over fear. I distinctly remember that my parents were surprised when they heard that they were having twins, especially since my mother was 44, and my dad was 56. That's extremely late to even have one baby…and two seemed like double the risk! I was 12 years old when my mother's water broke at 5 a.m., and my dad had to rush her to the hospital 20 miles away. I was left in charge of taking care of my younger sister, Roberta, and getting us both ready for the school bus.

We lived on 34 acres of land in Northern Michigan, which was very cold in the month of November, and very dark at 6 a.m.! I was afraid and literally shivering in my boots because I feared for my mothers well being while giving birth to twins. Nevertheless, it was my responsibility to care for my younger sister and get us safely on the bus that morning. I could not let my fear keep me from moving forward because not only was my sister counting on me, but so were my mom and dad. By the time my sister and I arrived at school, we heard the news on the small-town radio that my parents had a boy and a girl! It was a long recovery for my dear mother. My siblings, Zell and Zelika, are 62 years old now.

I'm so grateful that I didn't let my fears get the best of me that day on the way to school. Fear is a spirit that plays on our emotions and holds us back. The good news is that we have power over the spirit of fear. The phrase "do not be afraid" is written in the Bible 365 times. That's a daily reminder to live everyday free of fear. I've heard it said that fear is an acronym for False-Evidence-Appearing-Real. Another acronym for fear that gives me strength is; Face-Everything-And-Rise! Let your faith be bigger than your fears today. **2 Timothy 1:7** reads, *God has not given us a spirit of fear, but of power and of love and of a sound mind.* We can stand on the promises of God. So, whenever fear knocks on your door, send FAITH to answer!

Babs

Prayer: Dear Lord, I come before You to lay my fears at Your feet. Remind me of Your power and Your grace. Fill me with Your peace as I trust in You and You alone. I thank You for being my strength and my God in whom I trust, in Jesus' name. Amen!

"Stay In

Faith."

-Heather & Babs

DAY
9

Today I am grateful for...

_____
_____
_____
_____
_____
_____
_____

My thoughts...

_____
_____
_____
_____
_____
_____
_____
_____

Day 10

Dream, Pray, Write

Habakkuk 2:2
Write the vision and make it plain on tablets, that he may run who reads it.

I'm so glad that God knows the secret petitions of my heart. He knows every hidden dream and secret desire that I share with Him in my prayer time. I can dare to dream with God; big outrageous dreams like becoming a world-renowned inspirational speaker, author, talk show host, and health and fitness influencer. (Well, God did it for Oprah… Hey, I'd even take a red table talk, like Jada Pinkett-Smith.) These are the dreams that I hold close to my heart, take to God in prayer, and write down to remind myself that all God-given visions start with a written word. **Habakkuk 2:2** reads, ***Write the vision and make it plain on tablets, that he may run who reads it.*** It's easy as 1, 2, 3! Dream, Pray, Write!

We all get excited and want to share our deepest passions and dreams with our friends, family, and even strangers on social media. We must be careful about that. Even well-meaning people will discourage your dreams and have you thinking it's too late, you're too old, or that the world has enough book authors, public speakers, and inspirational women out there. Well, guess what? There's room for more! I've got a story to tell, and I'm going to tell it. As a matter of fact, I'm telling it right now!

This is how visions get started, with "Every Little Step" you take. And yes, I'm going to mention that's one of my favorite 90's jams by none other than New Edition's bad boy, Bobby Brown! So If 'you can't sleep at night…ya' toss and turn,' then it's time for you to dream again. It doesn't matter where you are in your life right now. It doesn't matter how much time was lost or how many mistakes you've made. Please remember that God's promises for your life are not confined by your failures, time, age, money, or any other limitations .Whether you've lost sight of a dream or you are daring to dream again for a fresh start, it's important for you to believe that it is possible. As the saying goes, "Shoot for the stars but if you happen to miss, shoot for the moon instead!"

Heather

Prayer: Dear Lord, I thank You that You bless me with dreams and visions of the plans that You have for me, and Your Word tells me that I don't have to fret or be anxious for anything, for You know exactly what You are doing. In Jesus name, Amen.

"Dream Big, Pray *Bigger.*"

-Heather & Babs

DAY 10

Today I am grateful for...

My thoughts...

Day 11

I Can See Clearly Now

John 9:6-7
When he had said these things, He spat on the ground and made clay with the saliva; and He anointed the eyes of the blind man with the clay. And He said to him, "Go, wash in the pool of Siloam." So he went and washed, and came back seeing.

For the longest time, my dear husband, Mark, had to suffer from sight impediment in one eye, because he had a detached retina that could not be repaired. Then, to make matters worse, a cataract began to form in his other eye impairing his vision to the point where it was almost completely gone. I knew that Jesus had healed blind people so many times during His earthly ministry, so I kept on believing and praying that He would somehow make a way for my husband to see again. Mark was afraid of cataract surgery because other doctors did not feel favorable about the out come.

To start, we tried every eye drop imaginable, but sadly, with no success. I worried that he would run out of time and lose his ability to see all together. And then, suddenly, God stepped in. One day when I was out of town, Mark called me in a state of panic, saying that he could barely even see the cell phone screen that was right there in front of him. I rushed home and took him to the emergency room. Thankfully, we made it to the hospital just in time. The surgeon said that his retina had also detached. As God would have it the surgeon not only attached the retina, but also removed the cataract as well, saving his vision!

I had no idea how God would heal Mark, but I had faith that it would happen. Sometimes we get discouraged because our prayers are not answered in the way that we envisioned. **John 9:6-7** reads, ***When he said these things, He spat on the ground and made clay with the saliva; and He anointed the eyes of the blind man with clay. And He said to him, "Go, wash in the Pool of Siloam." So he went and washed, and came back seeing.***

Jesus chose this method of healing. He put the best doctor in place to perform the miracle surgery. The oddness of the miracle, I think, speaks to its authenticity; and it shows the various means in which the Lord resolves difficulties in our lives. We must be open to God's creativity. When we see mud, Jesus sees miracles…Hey, Spit Happens!

Babs

Prayer: Dear Lord, I pray that You will comfort me and heal my loved ones. Give me such confidence in the power of Your grace that even when I am afraid, I may put my whole trust in You; in Jesus name, Amen.

"God's Timing Is *Perfect."*

-Heather & Babs

DAY 11

Today I am grateful for...

_____
_____
_____
_____
_____
_____
_____

My thoughts...

_____
_____
_____
_____
_____
_____
_____
_____

© LOOK ON THE BRIGHT SIDE

Day 12

Just Say No

Matthew 5:37
But let your 'Yes' be 'Yes', and your 'No', 'No.'

Billionaire CEO Warren Buffet once said, "The difference between successful people and really successful people is that really successful people say NO to almost everything!" When I read this, I knew I had some big changes to make if I wanted to accomplish my personal goals. I was that "eager to please" person, always going that extra mile. All the while, leaving little to no gas in my tank at the end of each day. This lil' car was running around on "E"!

I decided I wanted to start thinking more about myself and, how to secure my children's financial future. So, I said to myself, "What would be more exciting for a kid biz than selling freshly spun cotton candy?" So, I forged ahead and learned every single aspect of this venture, from marketing to packaging and even becoming the head sugar chef.

Most nights, the kids were fast asleep having sweet dreams while I was up late burning the midnight oil; setting off the smoke detectors as I taught myself how to operate a cotton candy machine. I now had a long list of things and people I had to say no to if I was going to focus my time and energy on our new business, Smart Cotton Candy. The whole incentive behind it was to save money for their college educations and to teach them at an early age how to be entrepreneurs.

I knew that God had given me this wonderful idea, and I wanted to be obedient to follow through and give it a try but, first I had to clear some things off my plate. Has God ever given you a dream, vision, idea, or assignment? Have you been putting it off because you are spread too thin while helping everyone else achieve *their* dreams?

What if your doctor was able to prescribe a miracle pill that promised to cure the "**Yes**-*itis*"? I would be the first in line with my co-pay to get mine. Since there is no such thing, I learned to slowly embrace the wisdom to only commit to what God was giving the green light.

Being too busy makes life imbalanced. I had to rise above the rush of endless demands and focus my time and energy on saying yes to God and no to man. **Matthew 5:37** reads, *But let your 'Yes' be 'Yes,' and your 'No,' 'No'*. Nobody's perfect, yet every believer should be accountable for everything we say and do. Our yes should be yes, and our no should be no—Periodt!

Heather

> **Prayer: Dear Lord, please guide my steps to show me how You want me to accomplish and achieve my goals. I pray for wisdom in all the decisions I make today. In Jesus name, Amen.**

"It's Ok To Say

No."

-Heather & Babs

DAY
12

Today I am grateful for...

My thoughts...

Day 13

Plant the Seed

1 Corinthians 3:6-7
I planted, Apollos watered, but God gave the increase. So then neither he who plants is anything, nor he who waters, but God who gives the increase.

One day while walking through the aisles of my favorite home away from home (Albertson's grocery store), I heard a young lady talking on her cell phone to one of her friends. As we were both in the cold fridge, and I was searching for pulp-free (never from concentrate) orange juice, I couldn't help but overhear her very personal conversation. She was extremely disappointed that a young man she was interested in was suddenly not returning any of her calls. She kept repeating, "I just don't understand. I thought our paths crossed for a reason."

When she got off the phone, I said to her, "Just keep a positive attitude and have faith that everything will work out." She said, "Oh, you must have read 'The Secret,' the book written about the law of attraction that everyone is talking about." I said, "No, I haven't, but I have read the

Bible, and I know there is no secret what God can do for you."

It didn't seem like that young lady totally understood what I was saying, yet I was just planting a seed. To plant a seed essentially means to lay the groundwork for something that can develop and bloom. **1 Corinthians 3:6-7** reads, *I planted, Apollos watered, but God gave the increase. So then neither he who plants is anything, nor he who waters, but God who gives the increase.*

What an honor it is for God to entrust us to be His fellow workers. We may never see when the seeds we plant grow and blossom to full potential but, if we do our part, God is faithful to do His. We cannot force someone to hear a message they are not ready to receive, but we must never underestimate the power of planting a seed.

Babs

Prayer: Dear Lord, I thank You for every individual that will labor in prayer. I honor You. You are my God, who will never fail me. May every seed I plant in faith yield a great harvest. In Jesus name, Amen.

"Grow Your

Faith."

-Heather & Babs

DAY 13

Today I am grateful for...

_____
_____
_____
_____
_____
_____
_____

My thoughts...

_____
_____
_____
_____
_____
_____
_____
_____

Day 14

It Never Rains

Romans 4:17
(as it is written, "I have made you a father of many nations") in the presence of Him whom he believed-God, who gives life to the dead and calls those things which do not exist as though they did.

The neo-soul sensation, Tony! Toni! Tone! sang one of my favorite songs back in the 90's, It Never Rains. Apparently, the crossover hit struck a chord with fans because the main chorus became an extremely popular coined phrase, "It never rains in Southern California!" How close to true is that statement, though? It hardly ever rains in Cali and when it does, it's a much-needed watering of land.

There was a pastor who told the members of his congregation one Sunday morning that he was very concerned about the serious drought in Southern California, and that they needed to come together in prayer regarding the matter. He asked them to meet within the following few days, and pray fervently that God would open the windows of heaven and pour out some water.

Next thing you know, Mother Molly walked through the church doors the day of the meeting with her gigantic umbrella in tote, a full-length raincoat, and some rain boots to match. The members were puzzled by her attire since the sun was out and shining brighter than a 90-watt light bulb! So, they asked her why she was dressed that way in the middle of August. She quickly replied, "Excuse me, but didn't the pastor say that we are gathered here to pray for rain? Well, I'm expecting God to make it rain. Y'all need to act as if it's already done and wait for God to move!"

Talk about demonstrating on the outside what you're believing for on the inside. I bet God was impressed with her tremendous faith. Are you dressed for success when it comes to the miracles you are believing God to perform in your life? Always remember that whatever it is that we're trying to achieve in life, we need to dress the part and act like it's already done. In other words, stay ready so you don't have to get ready.

Romans 4:17 reads, *(as it is written, "I have made you a father of many nations") in the presence of Him who he believed—God, who gives life to the dead and calls those things which do not exist as though they did.*

So, put on your galoshes with great expectation and watch God pour down a thunderstorm of blessings smack in the middle of your driest season.

Heather

Prayer: *Dear Lord, I am in expectation of a miracle today. Open the windows of heaven and let something big and outstanding happen quickly in my life, family, church, and nation. In Jesus name, Amen.*

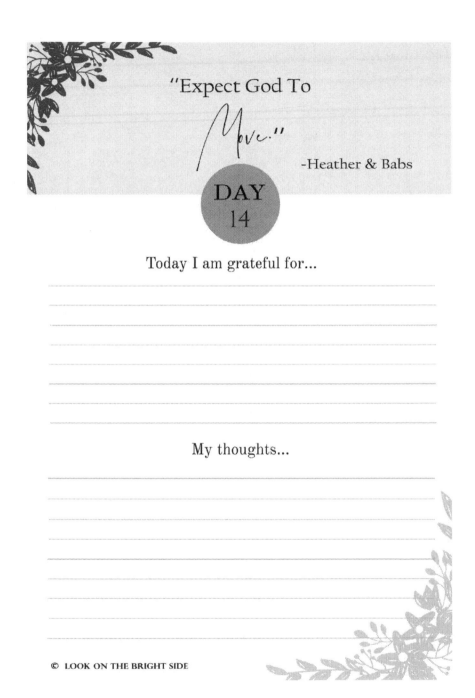

"Expect God To

Move."

-Heather & Babs

DAY
14

Today I am grateful for...

My thoughts...

Day 15

Aha! Moment

Jeremiah 29:11
For I know the thoughts that I think toward you, says the Lord, thoughts of peace and not of evil, to give you a future and a hope.

Oprah Winfrey once said, "It's not that I've always known who I would be. It was just very clear to me from an early age who I wouldn't be." When I was a young girl, my brother, Mack, and sister, Nicole had a discussion about their career goals, and what they aspired to be when they grew up. When they pondered what My life would amount to, they had low expectations, and came to the conclusion that they would purchase a teddy bear shop for me to run, because they couldn't envision what my purpose would be beyond playing with my stuffed animals all day. The struggle of living up to your siblings is real.

I admire those who know from an early age what gifts they possess and what they will contribute to society to better the world. I want to dream big and aim high in my career goals, while still being able to focus on my day job, with health benefits so that I can have stability and a means to care for my family.

As an adult, I made a decision that I did not want to work forever as an employee; year after year. Many of us work in a vocation that is not fulfilling and not in line with our purpose. After college, I moved to Los Angeles to pursue a career in television (the dream) while working in real estate management (the paycheck). Real estate management allowed me the opportunity to interact with residents. I am definitely a people person, yet this was not my ideal opportunity.

One day, feeling frustrated with my job, I asked God, "What would You have me do as my profession to glorify You and to walk in my purpose?" Once you ask God this bold question, be ready to leap out in faith when He answers you. While listening for God to answer, I was reminded of my 5th grade teacher, Mr. Benson, who told my mother that I was going to be a great writer one day.

This was when I had my Aha! moment. The birth of this book came from me asking God that simple question. "What I know for sure," (in my best Oprah voice) is that my purpose and greatest joy in life comes when I am able to be a blessing to others. Should this book encourage one person to go after their dreams, and to have a personal relationship with God, then I know that I am walking in my purpose.

God, who created us, gives us a personal promise to hold onto as a guarantee that our future will be bright.

Jeremiah 29:11 reads, *For I know the thoughts I think toward you, says the Lord, thoughts of peace and not of evil, to give you a future and a hope.* You may have been through some disappointments and tough times, but every experience whether positive or negative in your life is preparing you for what **He** has prepared *for* you! The Aha! moment, according to Oprah Magazine, is not somebody teaching you something. The Aha! moment is somebody helping you to remember. You can't have an Aha! moment unless you already knew it. Don't ever be afraid to pursue your purpose based on fear of failure. As Oprah once said, "Failure is another steppingstone to greatness. The biggest adventure you can ever take is to live the life of your dreams!"

Heather

Prayer: Dear Lord, may the dreams that You've deposited into my spirit continue to be revived until the time of their fulfillment. In Jesus name, Amen.

"Now I Get It,

Aha!"

-Heather & Babs

DAY
15

Today I am grateful for...

My thoughts...

Day 16

Are You Serious?

Ecclesiastes 3:4
A time to weep and a time to laugh; a time to mourn, and
a time to dance;

My son, Chris Jr., loves basketball and is the biggest Golden State Warriors & Steph Curry fan to ever walk the face of the earth. I remember ordering him a pair of basketball shoes online from Steph's highly anticipated Under Armour collaboration. From that moment forward I probably heard, "Did they come yet?" at least 1,000 times a Day! After the longest week of our lives, they finally arrived, and my son and I were both frantically opening that box up like Christmas decided to come early. When the smell of that leather hit my baby boy's nose, and the ocean water shade of blue glistened in his eyes, OH MY LORD! He was beaming from ear to ear! And guess what? So was I.

He almost tripped, running over to show his dad. But the first thing that daddy said with zero enthusiasm was, "Those are too big!" Talk about raining on my parade. I was thinking in my head what almost blurted out the side of my mouth, "Whaatt? Are you serious?! Excuse me, but we've been waiting close to forever for these pricey kicks to arrive, so I'm going to need EVERYBODY to bring their enthusiasm up a notch or two, Okurrr?!" My happy bubble was completed deflated. Even if the sneakers might have been a size too big, doesn't the Bible tell us to rejoice with those who rejoice?

Lets just say, I was annoyed with a capital "A". As for Chris Jr., he was as unbothered as he could be. What he said later that night gave me great wisdom. He said, "Oh well, Mom, the next time somebody doesn't respond the way you want, just laugh!" Wow, out of the mouth of babes. **Ecclesiastes 3:4** reads, *A time to weep and a time to laugh; a time to mourn and a time to dance;* Instead of fussing because things are not said or done the way we expect, brush it off with a giggle or two, and keep it moving.

Taking things too seriously when they really aren't all that big a deal will cost us the very things that are quite serious indeed...our peace and our joy. And who has time for that? I don't... well, not anymore! Life is too short to let little things bother us. Next time my husband decides to say something that's true but blue, I'll just give him a quick side-eye, exhale, and then laugh my little head off! I'm learning to live, love, and laugh, just like a child. Thanks, son.

Heather

> **Prayer: Dear Lord, help me to see the humor in my life. You said a cheerful heart makes good medicine. Thank You for helping me to laugh more often, in Jesus name, Amen.**

"Don't Burst My *Bubble.*"

-Heather & Babs

DAY 16

Today I am grateful for...

_____
_____
_____
_____
_____
_____
_____

My thoughts...

_____
_____
_____
_____
_____
_____
_____
_____

Day 17

Boss Baby

Job 23:10

***But He knows the way that I take; when He has tested me,
I shall come forth as gold.***

My ever so fickle acting career needed a plan b, and that plan b was a stable career working as an on-site residential property manager. I have had some tough and eccentric supervisors, but none of them compared to the one I secretly nicknamed, Boss Baby. He was fresh out of college, 12 years younger than me, and appointed to run the family business with little to zero know-how. Basically, he was playing monopoly with his daddy's millions and driving me crazy in the process.

Property management was not his thing, but instead of taking a quick crash course somewhere, he instead made poor decisions constantly, ones that I would have to reluctantly execute under his flawed leadership. He would micromanage me, challenge my EVERY move, demean me, call and nag me daily, and even nickel and dime me on building repair expenses. I worked for him for 10 years with

NO RAISE! Talkin' about, "She works hard for the money," (I feel you, Donna Summer!) Boss Baby kept me feeling quite frustrated, unappreciated, stressed, and full of work anxiety... but through all the test and trials, my consistent prayer to God was, "Lord, please remove him, or remove *me*!"

Then suddenly out of the blue, he announced that his family was selling the property. HALLELUJAH! (I tried not to look too happy.) My prayer was answered. Bye-bye, Boss Baby! I was over the moon that I would also be able to keep my same job, and would be transitioned into working for the new ownership. **Job 23:10** reads, *But He knows the way I take;. When He has tested me, I shall come forth as gold.* For gold to be tested, it must go through a refining process. The process requires fire so hot that it not only purifies the gold, it also allows the gold to be molded and transformed.

When you and I go through trials, just know that God is refining and transforming us into the best version of ourselves. God will step in and change the circumstance, change you, or change both. Either way, there's a blessing in your pressing, so keep praying and "Living Your Life Like it's Golden!" (Thanks, Jill Scott!)

Heather

Prayer: Dear Lord, I rebuke negativity today. Cover me under the precious blood of the Lamb. Infiltrate my mind, my body, and my soul. In Jesus name, Amen.

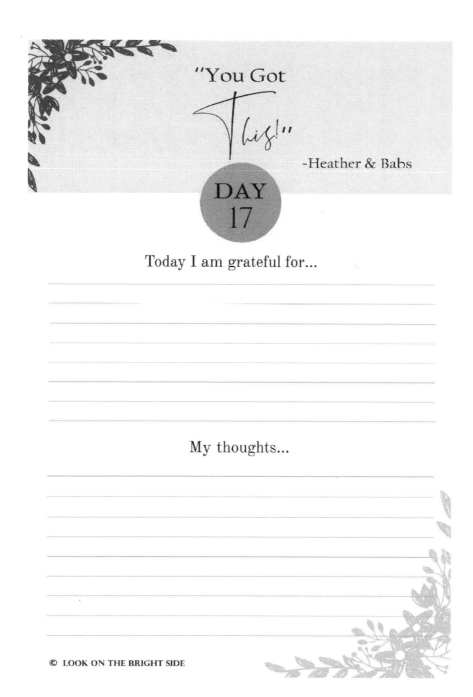

"You Got *This!*"

-Heather & Babs

DAY 17

Today I am grateful for...

My thoughts...

Day 18

Oops, I Did It Again

1 Corinthians 1:27
But God has chosen the foolish things of the world to put to shame the wise, and God has chosen the weak things of the world to shame the things which are mighty.

Throughout the course of history, God has woven certain people into His plan that may have made a mistake, or two that resulted in some larger-than-life outcomes. The Bible is filled with stories of people just like you, and me that have struggled, stumbled, failed and simply put, just messed up! As Brittany Spears once said, it's in these "Oops, I did it Again!" moments that the Lord teaches us His greatest lessons and He reveals His will along the way. It's also an opportunity to see the power of God's great mercy, forgiveness and grace.

Thank God that we have His word to remind us that the Bible is full of all kinds of questionable characters, yet none of their shenanigans kept God from using them while they were a messy work in progress. We learn that these were flawed people. They were far from perfect. In fact, they failed often. The men and women we read about are not there because they were great people; they are there because they had faith in a great God.

Consider some of the world changers mentioned in scripture. Abraham, the father of faith, lied about Sarah being his wife. Their son Isaac did the same thing. Sarah laughed at God's promise of a child and then denied she laughed. Isaac's son Jacob was a trickster. Samson was at times immoral, and Gideon was afraid. Rahab was a prostitute. David was an adulterer and a murder. Jonah ran from God. The disciples fell asleep while they were praying. The Samaritan woman was divorced more than once. Simon Peter openly denied the Lord, but God gave him a second chance. Noah had a drinking problem...and the list goes on and on.

Wow, sounds like a few characters from a modern-day soap opera or reality show, but this is all in the Bible. So what's your story? Think about it. These people all messed up, but God gave them a second chance. You can have a second chance, and God can use you. Maybe you feel like your story is over because of the mistakes you've made or a sin you've committed. Gospel music artist, Donnie McClurkin says it best in his song, "We Fall Down". The lyrics say, "We fall down but we get up...for a saint is just a sinner who fell down and got up." We all fall down, but get up and run again. Your story isn't over.

1 Corinthians 1:27 reads, *But God has chosen the foolish things of the world to put to shame the wise, and God has chosen the weak things of the world to put to shame the things which are mighty.* Through these stories we witness God's grace. We are able to see ourselves get past our mistakes, and do amazing things to give God glory. Their stories did not end in their sin; they ended in victory. So, let us take our messy lives to God who understands and has mercy. This is what redemption is all about!

Babs

Prayer: Dear Lord, continue to use me to do Your will. Continue to bless me so that I may be a blessing to others. Thank You for the victory today! In Jesus name, Amen.

"Be Of Good
Courage."

-Heather & Babs

DAY
18

Today I am grateful for...

_____
_____
_____
_____
_____
_____
_____
_____

My thoughts...

_____
_____
_____
_____
_____
_____
_____
_____

© LOOK ON THE BRIGHT SIDE

Day 19

Let It Go

Numbers 23:19
God is not a man that He should lie, Nor a son of man,
that He should repent. Has he said, and will He not do?
Or has He spoken, and will He not make it good?

I should have known when I got the call from my Aunt Z in Atlanta, playing long-distance matchmaker that this "dream" guy that she wanted to introduce me to was just too good to be true! According to the average woman's checklist, he was waaaay above average...tall, handsome, a NFL football player for the Baltimore Ravens, college graduate, never married and no children. He even purchased a dream home for his mom back in Texas. I mean, who can resist a guy who treats his mama great?! He'd come to visit me quite often in Cali, and yes, I fell for all his corny jokes, his cheesy charm, and his "wining and dining." Our first Christmas together, he even bought me a beautiful pearl and diamond ring!

One evening, he decided to join me for a mid-week service at my church, and he seemed to be listening rather attentively when the pastor was speaking about repentance. I reached down for a quick second to grab a mint out of my purse, and before I knew it he was rushing down to the altar to give his life to the Lord. Now it seemed like he truly was the full package. Little did I know that what had been concealed was about to be revealed.

He flew back to Atlanta and called me late that night. I figured he was calling to say he'd made it home safely, yet the Holy Spirit began to convict him to the point that he began blurting out, and confessing all the lies he had told me. It turned out he never played football for the NFL. He never graduated from Morehouse. He didn't own any homes or cars. He "had" a job working at Home Depot. When he kept constantly asking for time off to travel to Cali, they fired him. Remember that pearl and diamond-encrusted ring that he'd given me for my Christmas gift? That belonged to his ex-fiancé. He had the nerve to grab it out of her jewelry box as a "re-gift" to me since he could not afford to buy me a Christmas gift. I couldn't make this up if I tried!

Needless to say, I was devastated, hurt, embarrassed, mad, confused, disappointed, and so much more. **Numbers 23:19** reads, *God is not a man that He should lie, Nor a son of man, that He should repent. Has He said, and will He*

not do? Or has He spoken, and will He not make it good? Although I was disappointed, over time God allowed me to let go of my hurts and forgive him. One of my all time favorite country songs, "Unanswered Prayers"- by Garth Books says, "Sometimes I thank God for unanswered prayers…remember when your'e talkin' to the man upstairs that just because he doesn't answer doesn't mean he don't care…some of God's greatest gifts are unanswered prayers."

At the time I didn't understand this trial that I was going through, but now I know that God had my destiny in mind. He ended up being the very person who introduced me to my wonderful husband. Now that's a story for another time, but is that crazy or what? To God be the glory for the strangest plot twist imaginable. We've all had our share of relationship failures. Forgiving those who have wronged us is our gift to them. Having the strength to move on is our gift to ourselves!

Heather

Prayer: Dear Lord, today, I release everything that has tried to hinder or hold me back. I release the past. I release bitterness. I embrace Your grace and power to boldly move forward into the blessing You have for me. In Jesus name, Amen.

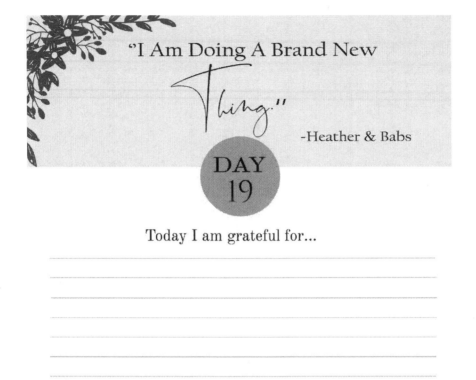

"I Am Doing A Brand New *Thing."*

-Heather & Babs

DAY 19

Today I am grateful for...

_____
_____
_____
_____
_____
_____
_____

My thoughts...

_____
_____
_____
_____
_____
_____
_____
_____

Day 20

A Kodak Moment

Psalms 126:5
Those who sow in tears shall reap in joy.

Long before Smartphones had these amazing built-in cameras, I still remember when Kodak introduced the pocket Instamatic camera way back in 1972. I clearly remember because this was the same year my youngest daughter, Heather, was born. As an adult, she often wondered why there were hardly any pictures of her as a baby. The truth is that snapping pictures was the absolute last thing on my mind at the time.

I was 27 years old, with three babies keeping me busy. All the while, I was desperately trying to save my marriage. I divorced in 1975, and consequentially, there are not many photos of Heather, who was a baby at the time. Things just did not work out for my marriage the way I had hoped. I remember when I cried that one night, wondering if things could have turned out differently had I made different choices. I prayed that one day my daughters would be blessed to have wonderful, supportive husbands.

Praise the Lord; my prayers were answered. Now that Heather is a mom, she is constantly taking pictures of my grandchildren, Savannah and Chris Jr. My daughter, Nicole and my son, Mack, also send me pictures of my grandchildren, Ellington and Heaven. It brings me great joy to know that they will look back on their childhood, and see all of the special moments that I was unable to capture amongst my own children.

I love the stanza from **Psalms 126:5**, It reads, ***those who sow in tears shall reap in joy.*** This scripture gives us great hope to know that God can make up for the pain and disappointments we've endured, and redeem the time. God's grace reverses our losses, and turns them into wins! Kodak Instamatic cameras are long gone, but today's moments are tomorrow's memories. Snapping pictures may not seem like a big deal now, but they will one day be priceless jewels. So, make sure you squeeze in plenty of time for taking pictures of practically any and everything your family does… and don't forget to include your *Selfie*!

Babs

Prayer: Dear Lord, thank You for reminding me that You are a deliverer. You are the one who came in and saved me from my past. Give me the strength to shift my focus on to the good part of my past. You are faithful. You are my help! In Jesus name, Amen.

"The Best Thing About
Memories Is Making
Them."

-Heather & Babs

**DAY
20**

Today I am grateful for...

My thoughts...

Day 21

Imma GOAL Digger

Philippians 4:8
Finally, bretheren, whatever things are true, whatever
things are noble, whatever things are just, whatever things
are pure, whatever things are lovely, whatever things are of
good report—if there is any virtue and if there is anything
praiseworthy—meditate on these things.

My grandma used to say that an idle mind is the devil's workshop! I really didn't understand what that meant as a child but when I became an adult I read this scripture. **Philippians 4:8** reads, *Finally, bretheren, whatever things are true, whatever things are noble, whatever things are just, whatever things are pure, whatever things are lovely, whatever things are of good report—if there is any virtue and if there is anything praiseworthy-meditate on these things.*

Oh! I see where she got that. The scripture urges us to keep our minds on things that are of a good report, so that we don't leave an open invitation for negative thoughts to fill our minds with all kinds of fears, and lies keeping us down and unproductive. We were created to be productive, so we won't let that happen.

One way that I keep my mind focused on good things, is by planning and pursuing my goals. I've given myself the nickname, <u>Goal</u> Digger (not to be confused with Kanye West's song, "Gold Digger"!) It makes me so happy to know that I can look forward to the benefits of seeing God manifest what was once a small idea in my mind into a real-life accomplishment! Setting goals gives us an internal accountability system, which helps us to stay focused and disciplined until our diligence finally pays off.

Your goals don't have to be gigantic, especially if you're new to making them. And trust me when you do the thrill of accomplishment will be so rewarding; you'll become an official Goal Digger also! I became motivated at an early age out of necessity. I realized quickly being raised by a single mom of three in the inner city of Detroit, that if I wanted to have some money for a cheerleading uniform, soccer cleats or a pair of acid wash Guess jeans (those were in at the time), I was going to have to have what my siblings and I call "The Hodges hustle!" (Hodges is my maiden name).

I was 14 at the time and the fact that most young adults started working at the age of 16 was not going to slow me down. When I found out there was this thing called a "work permit" that would allow me to start working ASAP, I applied for it immediately. I got my first job as an assistant manager of a singing telegram, balloon & cookie company in downtown Marietta, Georgia. It was called Happy Notes, and my #1 job description was to brighten the customers day as soon as they walked through the doors of this very small, but very festive gift shop. Who knew all these years later, I would be writing a book to encourage people in the same way? I've always been self-driven and self-motivated. I never had time for an idle mind because, just like Tupac said in his song, "I Get Around", I was too busy, "trying to make a dollar out of fifteen cents (a dime & a nickel!)"

Just because I had a long to-do list with a goal for this, and a goal for that didn't make me exempt from challenges, and the hard knocks of life. I had to learn how to stay focused on the goals and remember that it wasn't just good enough to have them. I had to put them into action and have faith in the end results. Maya Angelo says, "My mission in life is not merely to survive, but to thrive and to do so with some passion, some compassion, some humor and some style." And she sure did accomplish that mission and so much more! She was the epitome of a goal digger.

There is not a goal under the sun that God can't help you accomplish. While some are foolishly digging for the gold, let's be focused on chasing after the **goal**!

Heather

Prayer: Dear Lord, please give me inner wisdom and strength to overcome every obstacle. Help me focus on my creativity and to take care of myself physically, spiritually and mentally as I work toward my goals. Let all my achievements glorify You. In Jesus name, Amen.

"A Goal Without A Plan Is Just A

Wish."

-Heather & Babs

DAY
21

Today I am grateful for...

My thoughts...

Day 22

Giving Is Truly Living

Luke 6:38
Give, and it will be given to you: good measure, pressed down, shaken together, and running over will be put into your bosom. For with the same measure that you use, it will be measured back to you.

The Bible tells us it is more blessed to give than to receive! It wasn't until I got God's perspective on that truth that I was able to relish in the true pleasure of blessing other people. There is a benefit to making sure we live a life where our giving outweighs our receiving. After all, that's the formula for receiving MORE! More peace, more joy, more prosperity...it is endlessly yours if you give MORE. **Luke 6:38** reads, *Give, and it will be given to you: good measure, pressed down, shaken together, and running over will be put into your bosom. For with the same measure that you use, it will be measured back to you.*

Basically, you get what you give, and you reap what you sow. So, here's the deal, whatever you lack in your life, give it away. How can you give what you don't have? That's easy. There was a time when I wanted to start my own business, but did not have the resources. In that season, I began to plant seeds to help other entrepreneurs start their own businesses. A mommy friend needed extra income and wanted to start a business doing haircare for children. I gave her an idea for a very creative business name to get her started, "The Hair Nannie," and even sent her a few referrals so that she could build up her clientele.

I encouraged her dreams as I was still trying to find the courage and the resources for my own. If you don't have enough to meet your needs, then consider planting seeds! Need more love in your life? Start finding more ways to sow love into someone's life, and before you know it, your heart will be beaming with a joy you can't contain. You'll be, "So excited that you just can't hide it!" (Thanks, Pointer Sisters).

I love to give compliments. I can see someone wearing a cute pair of shoes and believe me, I'm the first one to say, "Gurl, I love those shoes!" I will find something nice to say to anyone. Giving is truly living, so, whether it's a verbal compliment, giving free advice, visiting seniors at a nursing home, serving at your church or volunteering in your local community, expect a return on your investment. Whatever you give from the heart, God will pay you back with interest!

Heather

> **Prayer: Dear Lord, I thank You, for blessing me and allowing me to wake up every day in good health and strength, but most importantly keeping me faithful to being a cheerful giver. I ask that You continue to bless me so I can be a blessing to others. In Jesus name, Amen.**

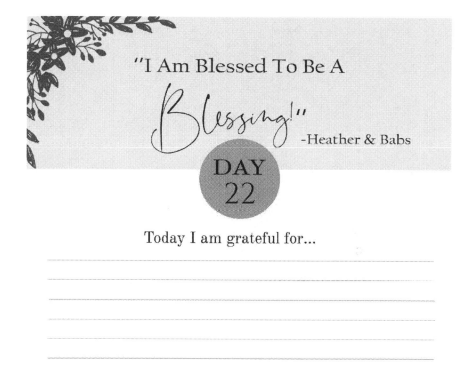

"I Am Blessed To Be A

Blessing!"

-Heather & Babs

DAY 22

Today I am grateful for...

My thoughts...

Day 23

Do – Over

1 John 1:9
If we confess our sins, He is faithful and just to forgive us our sins and to cleanse us from all unrighteousness.

Have you ever wished you could get a life do-over? What if we could just hit some magical reset button and could erase a mistake and get a second chance to make a different choice? Maybe you're having a tough time forgiving yourself. Well, here's the good news. If God can wipe the slate clean of an adulterous murderer, and bless him like it never happened, surely He can give you an opportunity to start over as well. Don't believe me? Then just keep on reading.

One day while Bathsheba was taking a bath up on a roof, King David got a glimpse of her beauty, and he could not stop staring! Instead of him minding his own business, closing his eyes and turning away, he sent his messengers into her home to bring her to his palace. Not only did King David know Bathsheba was married, but her husband was one of his most faithful soldiers! Nothing was stopping

King David from getting what he wanted from this bathing beauty.

Fast forward: Bathsheba gets pregnant; King David arranges for her husband to be killed on the front line of war, and they lost their first child at birth. Even so, God called King David "A man after My own heart." No matter how far off-track David got, he always came back to God with a quickness. While not perfect, he was a man who sought to live his life in obedience to the Lord; David responded with true repentance and humility after he had failed many times. Because of David's repentant heart, God blessed him and Bathsheba to conceive and bring forth another son, Solomon. This child later grew up to become a king! The same God who gave David another chance is willing and able to do the same for us. **1 John 1:9** reads, *If we confess our sins, He is faithful and just to forgive us of our sins and to cleanse us from all unrighteousness.* Allow God to take the mistakes of your past and weave them into an incredible future!

Babs

Prayer: Dear Lord, You are so merciful to me, and I am forever thankful for Your grace. Help me to walk in Your way. Create in me a clean heart, and renew a right spirit within me. In Jesus name, Amen.

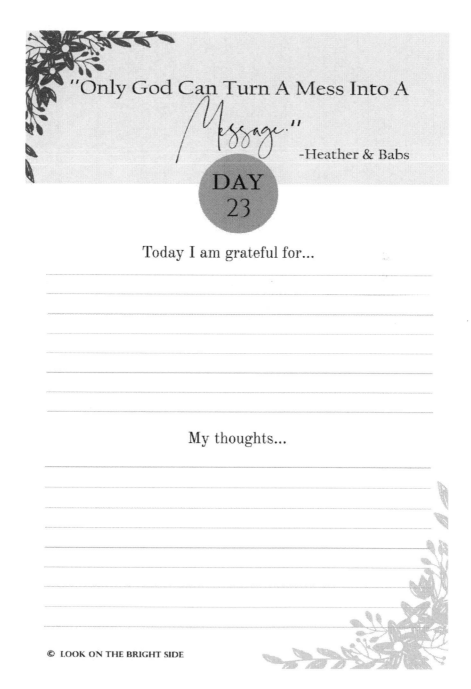

"Only God Can Turn A Mess Into A

Message."

-Heather & Babs

DAY
23

Today I am grateful for...

My thoughts...

© LOOK ON THE BRIGHT SIDE

Day 24

Encourage Her

Matthew 9:29

Then He touched their eyes, saying, "According to your faith, let it be done to you."

Growing up, Momma Babs was my biggest cheerleader. She made me think I was the most beautiful, talented, and smartest person in the entire world. With a mustard seed of faith, nothing would be impossible for me in her eyes. In high school, I was bringing home grades like C's, sometimes even D's, but mom would still greet me with a big hug and encourage me to keep on trying. She was always so excited to encourage me no matter what the report card said. Because of her encouragement my grades actually got better!

Now I see myself doing the same thing with my children. I am constantly uplifting, motivating, and supporting my children in whatever goal they are working towards. I remember Savannah's first elementary talent show when she had to perform a solo dance in front of hundreds of people. I styled her in the perfect sparkly performance outfit, and as we rehearsed nightly, I encouraged her that if she put in the practice and hard work, she was going to be amazing dancing across that stage…and that she was!

My children showed interest in being in the entertainment business. I remember reaching out in faith to email the top three talent agencies in Los Angeles in hopes of getting representation for both of my children. I had my momma's mustard seed faith on the inside of me. And guess what? One of those top three agents emailed me that same evening, saying they'd love to meet my children.

So far, Savannah booked the Nickelodeon's Kids Choice Sports Awards and an AT & T print ad. Chris Jr. is now a member of the Screen Actors Guild, and has had great success on national commercials and even a guest spot on the ABC show, The Bachelorette! We are now setting our sites on more television and film because there is no limit.

Whatever it is you're believing God for, just know that you've got this. We are here to encourage you, and cheer you on. In God's eyes, there is nobody greater than you. The Bible reads in **Matthew 9:29**, *Then He touched their eyes, saying, "According to your faith, let it be done to you".* Faith is daring the soul to go beyond what eyes can see. Believe it, conceive it, take steps to achieve it. Then leave the rest to God and prepare to receive it!

Heather

> **Prayer: Dear Lord, make me an encourager today. You lifted me up, so let me also lift others in the spirit of encouragement and hope. Grant me an opportunity to help others find the strength and the courage to use their gifts according to Your master plan. In Jesus name, Amen.**

"Focus On The

Good."

-Heather & Babs

DAY
24

Today I am grateful for...

_____
_____
_____
_____
_____
_____
_____

My thoughts...

_____
_____
_____
_____
_____
_____
_____

Day 25

Extreme Scream

Isaiah 26:3
You will keep him in perfect peace, whose mind is stayed on You, Because he trusts in You.

Raising children of any age can feel like being on a roller coaster ride at Magic Mountain! With so many twists and turns, unexpected ups and downs, and jolting moments that make you want to scream, sometimes you just want to throw your hands in the air and yell, "LET. ME. OFF. THIS. THING. NOW!" Have any of you parents ever felt like that? I'm glad I'm not alone. I think we can all agree that, even with all of the crazy, scary, time to freak out moments we experience, we would still go back and stand in a line for however long it takes to have the most exhilarating adventure of a lifetime over and over again… Parenthood!

I have a pre-teen daughter, so most of my conversations with her are filled with statements like, "Pick your clothes off the floor, wash your face, quit eating toxic Takis, brush your teeth, make your bed, smooth your edges, drink water, don't add sugar to Frosted Flakes, don't talk back, fix ya face, don't wear half tops, hug your brother, read your Bible, read a book, get off of your iPhone, don't overstuff your mouth with food, make eye contact," etc., etc., and more etc's!

One particular day, I was piling on the critiques a bit too heavy (you know, the kind you meant to help but they really don't.) when God reminded me of what my Grandma Alma taught me. She said, "Words can hurt or heal, what did your words do today?" Ugh, she was so right. I'm now learning to speak life into my baby girl by praising her for what she does well, and I take my issues of concern to God in prayer, who can do a much better job at both molding her, and transforming her to His will . I'm also making sure I take the time to read the Bible with her. Of course, she'd rather be making a Tiktok video, doing the newest online dance challenge, watching YouTube or chatting it up with her besties on Snapchat, but Momma has to make sure her future goals are grounded in the purpose of her Heavenly Father! Worrying about the well-being of our children often feels like the ultimate tummy drop! **Isaiah 26:3** reads, *You will keep him in perfect peace whose mind is stayed on You, Because he trusts in You.*

Trust God with your children, and you will be in peace. Keep your mind on what He says and not what you see. Otherwise, we will be too stressed to be blessed and will turn our children into nervous wrecks. Yes, I still belt out the occasional scream and will shed more than a tear or two on the upside-down, curving and swerving loopty loops of the "for parents only" ride of no return. My seatbelt is tight and secure in Jesus. I have a grip on His promises, and I'll be ready for one more ride when it's all over! After all, we didn't just sign up for the annual pass. This is the adventure of a lifetime, and this membership does not include the Fast Pass!

Heather

> **Prayer: Dear Lord, I lift every child to You for Your blessings and guidance. Lord, order their footsteps as they walk on their own. I declare that they will set an example for believers in speech, in conduct, in love, in faith and in purity. I pray that You keep our children on Your righteous path so that their lives may be an example to all around them. In Jesus name, Amen.**

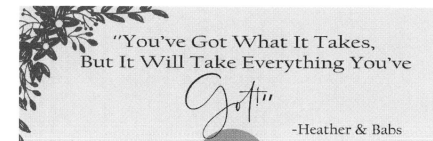

"You've Got What It Takes,
But It Will Take Everything You've

Got!"

-Heather & Babs

**DAY
25**

Today I am grateful for...

My thoughts...

Day 26

Cares Fluffed and Folded

1 Peter 5:7
Casting all your care upon Him, for He cares for you.

If the local Fluff and Fold laundromat promised that you could drop off ALL your dirty laundry for their staff to happily wash it, iron it and fold for FREE, wouldn't you gladly let them do it? Or, would you keep going back several times during the week to check on your loads, to pick through your dirty laundry and take some pieces back home with you before they've been cleaned? Wouldn't the Fluff and Fold staff be giving you the side-eye, wondering why you didn't just wait until the job was completed?

I wonder if that's how God feels when we take our dirty laundry (cares & worries) to prayer, and we say, 'Fix it, Jesus!' At that moment we believe that He will. Just like the laundry story if our prayers are not answered instantly do we stop trusting God, and begin taking these concerns back to try to fix them on our own ?

1 Peter 5:7 reads, *Casting all your care upon Him, for He cares for you.* That literally means dump every load that you have (even if it's filthy and stained) right at the feet of Jesus and allow Him to clean it all up as only He can. God is saying, "Give me your whites and colors, give me the all bulky items and the delicates, even the special dry clean only items. I'll carry and clean all your heavy loads." Jesus is the stain remover for the mess our sin creates.

Unlike the local Fluff and Fold, He may not have all your problems solved and ready for pick by next Friday at noon. Remember that God's timing is perfect, but you have to trust Him. Worrying is like telling God that you don't think He can handle your problems and concerns. Trust me; He can handle it.

One of my favorite Kirk Franklin songs is called, "He Can Handle It." The lyrics say, "He can handle it…There's no doubt about my Savior…I know He will deliver…He can… handle it…whatever it is…He can handle it." He promises that if we trust Him, His peace that passes all understanding will flood our mind as we put our trust in Him. If you find yourself worrying about that thing again, stop right in your tracks and say, "Whatever it is…He can handle it!"

Heather

> *Prayer: Dear Lord, help me not to worry about tomorrow but instead focus on what You're doing in my life right now. I want to trust in Your promise to take care of every one of my needs (financial, relational, physical, social, spiritual, and emotional). Help me to trust You more and worry less, I pray. In Jesus name, Amen.*

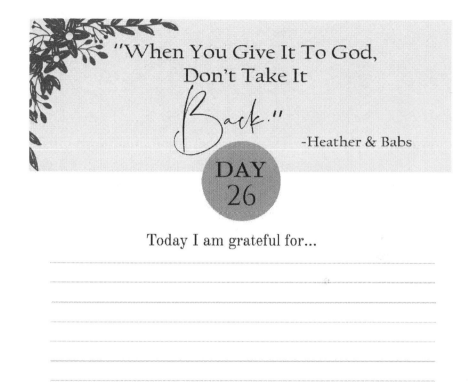

"When You Give It To God,
Don't Take It

Back."

-Heather & Babs

**DAY
26**

Today I am grateful for...

My thoughts...

Day 27

The Other Woman

Proverbs 3: 13-14
Happy is the man who finds wisdom, and the man who
gains understanding; For her proceeds are better than the
profits of silver, And her gain than fine gold.

I don't consider myself a nosey person, but this particular morning, while I was making the bed and tidying up the bedroom, I stumbled upon my husband's open journal. When I glanced and read the title, "Her," I couldn't help but be curious. This is what he wrote:

I have to have her. She is comforting. She's discreet. She gives good advice. She's beautiful. She's not biased to gender, race, or your economic status. She's a reminder of things without nagging. She can be fierce and sweet at the same time. She wears multiple hats without looking awkward. She's comfortable being kept a secret. She won't deal with fools because they won't appreciate her. She has much to offer, including enduring wealth, prosperity, and life to anyone who would heed her words. She is more precious than rubies, and all the things you may desire cannot compare with her.

The best part is that I know my wife doesn't mind me having her. Her name is WISDOM.

Wheew! I was so relieved to hear about this lady Wisdom and nobody else! I brewed my morning pot of coffee extra strong and added a double shot of vanilla creamer to take the edge off my nerves. Then I sat down and began to study more about "Her." The word wisdom is mentioned 222 times in the Bible. There is also reference to wisdom personified in female form.

The Bible tells us that wisdom is more than just a benefit or a characteristic. Wisdom is sometimes a person. When so personified, wisdom is always a woman. Sometimes she is Lady Wisdom. Sometimes she is Madame Insight. Most often, she goes incognito, yet the shadow she casts is always a female form. **Proverbs 3:13-14** reads, *Happy is the man who finds wisdom, and the man who gains understanding; For her proceeds are better than the profits of silver, And her gain than fine gold.* I will be sure to tell my husband that I found out about "Her," and that she's a keeper!

Heather

Prayer: Dear Lord, thank you for Your wisdom and understanding. Allow me to discern and recognize the people You have divinely placed in my life who speak holy truth, love and words of wisdom. In Jesus name. Amen.

"I Choose To Be

Wise."

-Heather & Babs

DAY 27

Today I am grateful for...

_____
_____
_____
_____
_____
_____
_____

My thoughts...

_____
_____
_____
_____
_____
_____
_____
_____

© LOOK ON THE BRIGHT SIDE

Day 28

Living In A Material World

Matthew 6:33
But seek first the kingdom of God and His righteousness,
and all these things shall be added to you.

Madonna's song, "Material Girl," may have been a smash hit back in the 80's, but the title alone still speaks to the state of society today more than ever before. We want it all, and smartphones are picking up on even the slightest leads when we as consumers are tempted to spend money shopping online. I recall recently that before I could even finish typing the "s" in mattress, my phone was lit up with bed advertisements from here to Timbuktu! With easy credit line approvals and pay as you go installment options (with high interest rates), it's so hard to resist the temptation of buying the things you want vs. the things you actually need. It takes a lot of discipline and prayer to not get caught up. Some days I try to beat my husband home to save myself the embarrassment of explaining the large collection of Amazon Prime box deliveries on our front doorstep.

My sister Nicole was 24, and I was 21 when we jumped on that Greyhound bus with dreams of pursuing our acting careers. We said, "Goodbye, Marietta, Georgia" and "Here we come, Californ-i-ayyye!" Television shows like, The Cosby Show and A Different World had inspired two sister dreamers to make that big move to the West Coast. If we wanted to make our dreams a reality, Cali was the place to be.

All we wanted was to be L.A. "It" girls with the designer handbags and have that glamourous Hollywood lifestyle we saw on tv. (Ok, maybe my sister was legit studying theater, working on her master's degree at UCLA and honing her acting craft), but I just wanted to know if Melrose Place was a real address where we could take up residence!

Our first apartment was a dinky little one-bedroom in "Miracle" Mile (we took that as a sign.) and between the both of us, we couldn't even scrape together our $575 monthly rent, and that included utilities. I remember calling my big brother, Mack, back in Atlanta saying, "send more money. Any day now, our auditions and networking are going to pay off. We're getting closer to our big Hollywood break; wait and see." He was all in, sending money monthly and 100% confident that we were the next big stars.

Our first acting parts were on tv shows like Martin, Roc and Sister, Sister! We were extras (the folks that fill in the background) making minimum wage basically, but you couldn't tell us nothin'. We were so excited to be on these sitcoms that we lost our minds in the process. We would take the money we earned or borrowed and, instead of securing the place where we laid our heads, we would go and spend it on new outfits, complete with fake designer handbag. All this so we could "look the part."

We soon learned that we were going to have to get a night job to support our day dream. Those were hard lessons to learn. We would endure hard times, splitting meals at Norm's family restaurant, sleeping on furniture we bought at yard sales, purchasing a "lemon" from a non-reputable car dealer called, "Cars Yes;" boy... I sure wish we would have just said No!

Times got tough, and we were missing our mom and family back home in Georgia. There were times when we thought of giving up and moving back, but God had a plan. A few Hollywood friends would eventually lead us to The Bible Enrichment Fellowship Church in Inglewood, CA, where we gave our lives to Christ and became born again believers. Life began to shift for us at that point. When we were focusing on the material things of this world to make us happy, we found ourselves disappointed. We travelled all the way to Cali to learn that true joy is in Jesus!

It's ok to want the finer things in life but there was an order and priority to things, I had to learn that. Life lessons have taught me it's all about living a balanced life and seeking God first in everything. Back then, I made what I thought were "good" decisions but not necessarily "God" decisions, since I didn't have the knowledge to seek Him first for direction. **Matthew 6:33** reads, *But seek first the kingdom of God and His righteousness, and all these things shall be added to you.* I had a good heart and good intentions, but I was living out of order. I had to learn how to seek the kingdom of God and His righteousness **first** before all these other "things" would be added onto me. We surely are living in a material world. Madonna got that part right. But I am no longer a material girl. It turns out that it's actually the spiritual world that has made me rich!

Heather

Prayer: Dear Lord, please forgive me for loving things and placing them over You. Forgive me for those times that I was not a good steward of Your blessings. Help me to always seek You first! In Jesus' name. Amen.

"*Live*

Life More Abundantly."

-Heather & Babs

DAY
28

Today I am grateful for...

_____

_____

_____

_____

_____

_____

_____

My thoughts...

_____

_____

_____

_____

_____

_____

_____

_____

© LOOK ON THE BRIGHT SIDE

Day 29

Put God 1st

Philippians 4:6-7
Be anxious for nothing, but in everything by prayer and
supplication, with thanksgiving, let your requests be made
known to God; and the peace of God, which surpasses all
understanding, will guard your hearts and minds through
Christ Jesus.

The key to having an abundant life full of God's love, peace and joy, is keeping Him in His rightful place in our priorities. I love the Lord and always put Him first. I do my best to devote some early morning time to chatting it up with Jesus because after all, as my friend, I can share both my concerns and my wants with Him. From my bills to my ills, He is there with all ears.

Before I made a conscious decision to put God 1st in the morning when I awake, there were many days I'd start my day feeling overwhelmed, with the cares of life weighing me down. As soon as I let my feet hit the floor, I'd be running a mile a minute and couldn't seem to get it all in! That's because I wasn't allowing God to order my steps.

Whatever may be troubling me, I know without a shadow of a doubt that it can be solved by remembering these most reliant words. **Philippians 4:6-7** reads, *Be anxious for nothing, but in everything by prayer and supplication, with thanksgiving, let your requests be made known to God; and the peace of God, which surpasses all understanding, will guard your hearts and minds through Christ Jesus.*

Making time for God must be our first priority. Everything else can wait. Also, starting our day with plenty of gratitude is bound to change our attitude. Make a list each morning of all the things that make you feel grateful. Try spending at least 15 minutes each day in prayer. God speaks to those who take time to listen, and He listens to those who take time to pray.

Heather

> *Prayer: Dear Lord, help me to lean not on my own understanding but on the infinite wisdom You have prepared for me. I pray that You remind me of just how blessed I am and that You never allow me to forget to show my gratitude in prayer. In Jesus name, Amen.*

"Start Your Day With

God."

-Heather & Babs

**DAY
29**

Today I am grateful for...

My thoughts...

© LOOK ON THE BRIGHT SIDE

Day 30

Taming the Tongue

Ephesians 4:29
Let no corrupt word proceed out of your mouth, but what is good for necessary edification, that it may impart grace to the hearers.

It was a Friday evening, and I was waiting ever so patiently for a parking space outside of our favorite hot wing spot. As soon as a space opened, another car came quickly swooping in from behind and into MY spot. I had a car full of kids (mine, along with a few more), who were watching how I would handle that situation. So, after rolling down my window and expressing how rude that was, I could see that my son was nervous about getting into a confrontation.

I had to really control my flesh and practically bite my own tongue because it took everything in me not to go off. I had a cloud of witnesses in the car and in that moment, I decided to let Jesus take the wheel because, I was not about to explain to the kids how I'm a Christian but I cuss a little when under pressure, lol! That is not a good look. We want our lifestyle and our conduct to be pleasing to God. Saying yes to God by yielding to His will is positioning us to say no to a lot of the nonsense we may have entertained in the past. "Knowing" God's word allows us to begin "No"ing (saying no to) the things of the world like ungodly behavior and unflattering speech. **Ephesians 4:29** reads, *Let no corrupt word proceed out of your mouth, but what is good for necessary edification, that it may impart grace to hearers.* We need the word of God in our lives to help remind us of the importance of speaking life to ourselves and others.

When we know better, we should do better. Our flesh has a mind of its own, but as we begin to get the word of God in our spirit, it helps us to tame our tongue. Once you know the truth about who you are in Christ, you are now responsible to turn away from bad habits, sin, certain people, certain places, bad language, and even our thoughts that are not pleasing to God. Then, we are able to transform our lives and make a positive impact on our future. People are always watching, and more importantly, so is God. Don't look at what people say, look at what they do. Actions speak louder than words. As our dear Bishop Dillard would say, "We should always witness, and sometimes use words."

Heather

Prayer: Dear Lord, I know my tongue often gets ahead of my mind and heart. Please help me see when I am about to speak without thinking and to check my heart. Help me be slow to speak. Help me, Lord, to be a person full of loving words, full of Your Spirit, overflowing with love, joy, peace, patience, kindness, gentleness and self-control. In Jesus name, Amen.

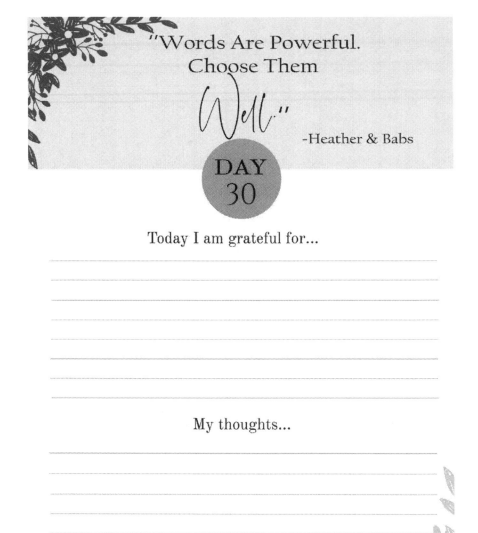

"Words Are Powerful.
Choose Them
Well."

-Heather & Babs

**DAY
30**

Today I am grateful for...

My thoughts...

© LOOK ON THE BRIGHT SIDE

Day 31

VIP Invitation

Romans 10:9-10
That if you confess with your mouth the Lord Jesus and
believe in your heart that God has raised Him from the
dead, you will be saved. For with the heart one believes
unto righteousness, and with the mouth confession is made
unto salvation.

Some say that they don't attend church because they never get an invitation. I remember the day I accepted an invite from a friend to attend a church service in Inglewood, CA. On the way to church I will never forget a Kirk Franklin song that came on the radio, "Why We Sing." Those lyrics moved me to tears because I was ready for a change in my life. The lyrics said, "Someone asked a question, why do we sing? When we lift our hands to Jesus... what do we really mean? Someone may be wondering when we sing our song, at times we may be crying...and nothings even wrong...I sing because I'm happy...I sing because I'm free..His eye is on the sparrow ...that's the reason why I sing...Glory Hallelujah...You're the reason why I sing."

That day in church I gave my life to the Lord and my life changed forever. I am so grateful that I said yes to the invitation. You have probably received a lot of invitations in your lifetime. I'm sure you've attended some amazing birthday parties, graduations, and even wedding receptions. Those are some great parties to attend, but the greatest invitation you will ever receive is the Holy Spirit inviting you to have a personal relationship with God. **Romans 10:9-10** reads, *That if you confess with your mouth the Lord Jesus and believe in your heart that God has raised Him from the dead, you will be saved. For with the heart one believes unto righteousness, and with the mouth confession is made unto salvation.*

On the following page you will find your personal invitation to God's Big Party (and since you are a **V**ery **I**mportant **P**erson to God… that means that you are on the **VIP** List!) We want to encourage you to share this invitation with EVERYONE you meet because it's not just the party of the year…it's the party of an eternal lifetime! We really hope to see you there!

Heather & Babs

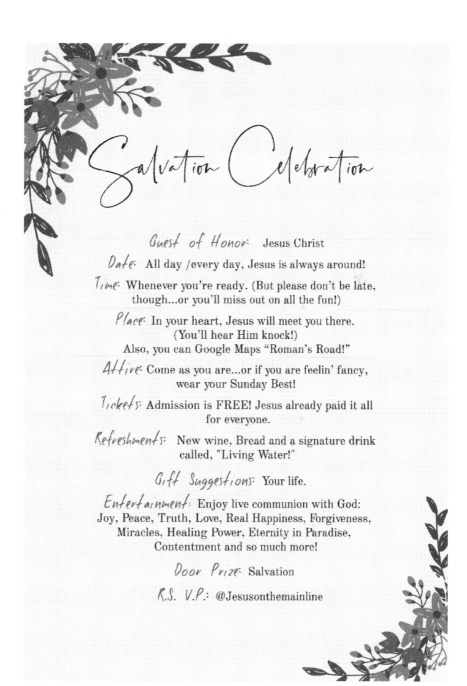

Salvation Celebration

Guest of Honor: Jesus Christ

Date: All day /every day, Jesus is always around!

Time: Whenever you're ready. (But please don't be late, though...or you'll miss out on all the fun!)

Place: In your heart, Jesus will meet you there.
(You'll hear Him knock!)
Also, you can Google Maps "Roman's Road!"

Attire: Come as you are...or if you are feelin' fancy,
wear your Sunday Best!

Tickets: Admission is FREE! Jesus already paid it all
for everyone.

Refreshments: New wine, Bread and a signature drink
called, "Living Water!"

Gift Suggestions: Your life.

Entertainment: Enjoy live communion with God:
Joy, Peace, Truth, Love, Real Happiness, Forgiveness,
Miracles, Healing Power, Eternity in Paradise,
Contentment and so much more!

Door Prize: Salvation

R.S. V.P.: @Jesusonthemainline

The Prayer to receive the Gift

The scripture says, "Whoever calls upon the name of the Lord will be saved." If you would like to know Christ, all you have to do is receive the free gift of salvation through Jesus Christ by saying a prayer of salvation. Pray this aloud, "Lord Jesus, I repent of my sins. Come into my heart. Wash me clean. I make you my Lord and Savior, Amen." We believe that if you prayed that simple prayer you have been born again. You are starting with a clean slate, and you have entered into a personal relationship with Jesus Christ. Keep God first place in your life. Learn to pray. Prayer is simply talking to God like you would talk to a friend. Mark today's date, write it down in your Bible, this is the day of new beginnings in your life!

List of the Scriptures in the order they appear:

Matthew 5:16

Proverbs 17:22

Matthew 6:34

Mark 11:25

Psalms 130: 4

Psalms 149: 3

Genesis 2:2

Ecclesiastes 3:1

Psalms 28:7

Psalms 118:8

2 Timothy 1:7

Habakkuk 2:2

John 9:6-7

Matthew 5:37

1 Corinthians 3:6-7

Romans 4:17

Jeremiah 29:11

Ecclesiastes 3:4

Job 23:10

1 Corinthians 1:27

Numbers 23:19

Psalms 126: 5

Philippians 4:8

Luke 6:38

1 John 1:9

Matthew 9:29

Isaiah 26:3

1 Peter 5:7

Proverbs 3:13

Matthew 6:33-34

Philippians 4:6-7

Ephesians 4:29

Romans 10:9-10

About the Mother Daughter Authors

Heather Bourne is the wife of Pastor Christopher Λ. Bourne, Senior Pastor of Second Baptist Church-Monrovia, CA for 16 years. She is a mother of two Savannah 13, Chris Jr. 10, a television host, inspirational speaker, author, and CEO of Smart Cotton Candy. Lady Heather has an AA degree in Liberal Arts from LACC and is working on her Bachelor's degree in Business Management at WGU. She has worked in real estate management while pursuing a career in television and film for over 20 years. She is Barbara's youngest daughter who loves being a wife and mom, shopping, gospel music, serving others, taking naps and home- made pound cake.

Barbara Westmaas is a wife, mother of 3, author of (Mama Said) and a proud "Glam"ma to four grandchildren. Barbara has a BA in Psychology from the University of Michigan. She is retired but continues to work part time as a life coach and author. She loves nature, spending time with her grandchildren, shopping on HSN, keeping up with the latest dance moves, and strawberry shortcake (made with Heather's homemade pound cake.)

For speaking engagements, please contact the authors at:

lookonthebrightsidebook@gmail.com
@lookonthebrightsidebook

Look on the Bright Side

Made in the USA
Columbia, SC
06 June 2021

39219753R00080